Slippery, Slimy

BABY FROGS

Sandra Markle

Walker & Company ✹ New York

You may not have seen a baby frog like this Monkey Tree Frog baby from Peru. But frogs live in all parts of the world except Antarctica. So nearly everywhere, baby frogs of one kind or another can be spotted in streams, in ponds, in puddles—even in tiny pools of water trapped in a plant's leaves. They can also be found in a foam nest in a tree, in a pouch on their mother's back, or inside their father's mouth. So how does a baby frog live? How does it stay safe? And what kinds of changes happen as it grows up? This book gives you a close look at baby frogs—also known as "tadpoles."

Frogs belong to a group of animals called *amphibians* (am-FIB-ee-anz). The name means "leading two lives." They're called that because adult frogs and baby frogs look and behave very differently. Adults, like this Gray Tree Frog, can stay out of water at least part of the time. That's why adult frogs are built to jump as well as swim. And adults have *lungs* to extract *oxygen,* the gas they need to live, from the air.

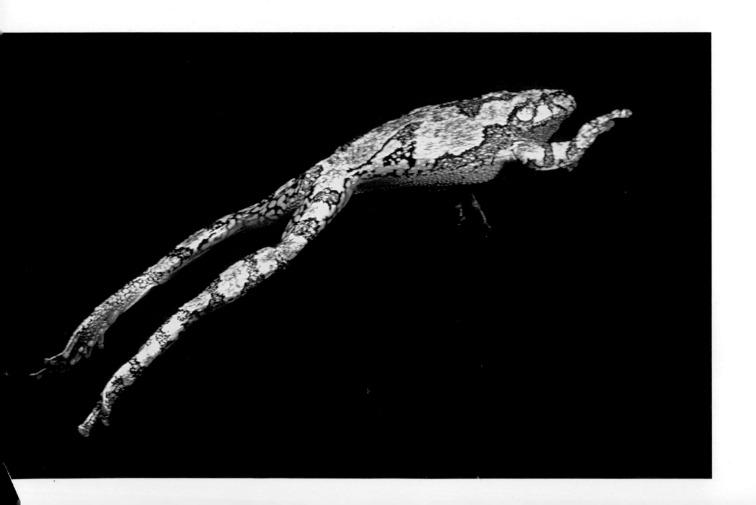

Baby frogs, like this Red-eyed Tree Frog tadpole, can live only in water. That's why tadpoles are fish-shaped—to be good swimmers. Like fish, baby frogs also have *gills* to extract the oxygen they need from the water.

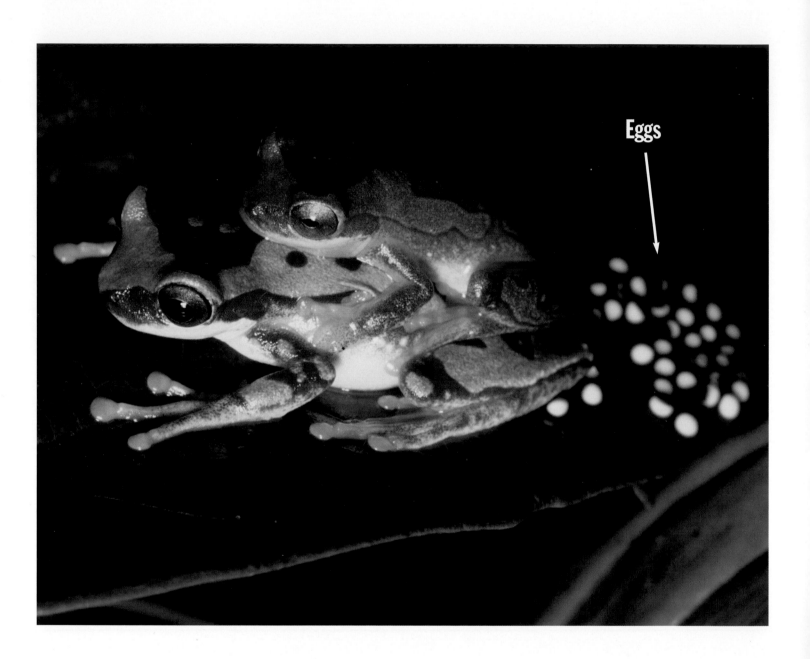

Eggs

STARTING LIFE IN AN EGG

These Hourglass Tree Frogs are mating. To produce babies, a female frog lays *eggs*. Then the male covers the eggs with a liquid containing special cells, called *sperm*. When a sperm merges with an egg, a baby frog starts to develop.

Each newly laid frog egg is inside a jellylike blob. The outer surface of this jelly forms a rubbery shell. But water is able to pass through this shell. When the jelly gets wet, it quickly swells to nearly twice its size. This thick layer of jelly becomes a protective covering for the egg. It keeps the egg from being bumped and from getting too hot or too cold. As long as the jelly stays wet, it also lets oxygen pass through to the developing baby frog. Even inside the egg, the baby frog needs oxygen to live and grow. So frog parents make sure their eggs stay wet.

Many frogs, like Bullfrogs, keep their eggs wet simply by laying them in water. Other frogs, like these Foam Nest Frogs, produce a special coating to keep their eggs from drying out. Foam Nest Frogs mate in a group up in a tree. During mating, the females give off a thick, sticky liquid and whip it with their hind legs until it's like stiff egg whites. The females deposit their eggs inside the group's foam nest. Soon the surface of the foam hardens into a protective case. This keeps the eggs inside moist and soft. Because the foam bubbles contain trapped air, there is a supply of oxygen for the developing babies.

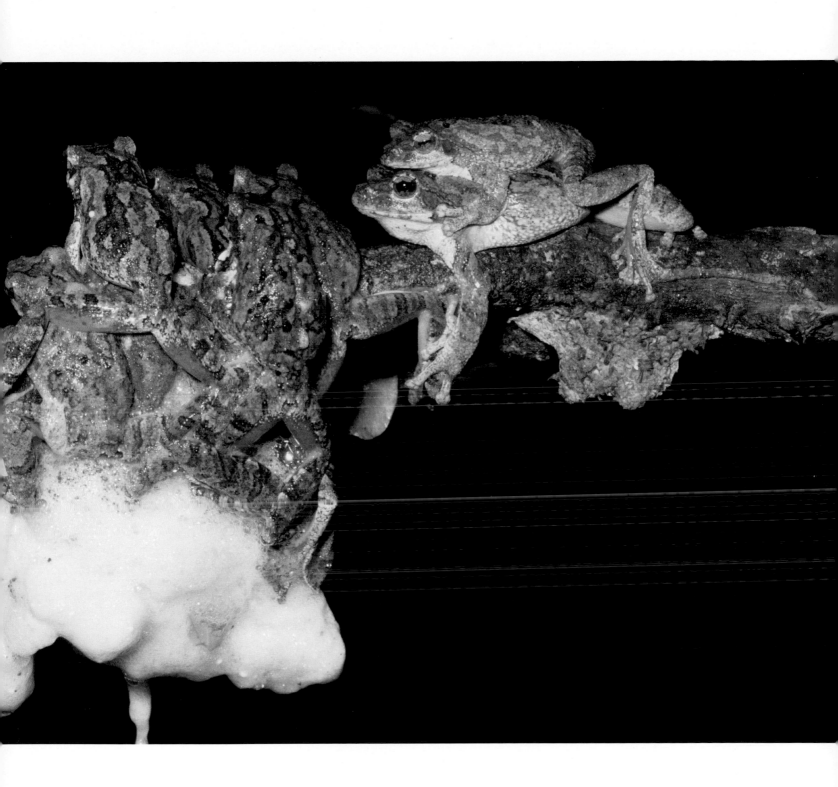

Some frogs, like this *Phrynopus* (fry-NOP-us) female, lay their eggs on the ground in a place that's nearly always damp, like under moss. She stays nearby, regularly peeing on the eggs to keep them wet while the babies develop.

Pygmy Marsupial (PIG-mee mar-SOOP-e-ul) Frogs have a special way to keep their eggs wet. The lumps on this female Pygmy Marsupial Frog's back are her eggs. When she mated, the male frog coated the eggs with sperm and pushed them into a pouch on her back. Now, while she goes about finding food and staying safe, the *mucus* produced by her *skin* keeps the eggs wet.

Many kinds of frogs don't stay with their eggs or guard them. So those frog parents usually produce lots of eggs. Bullfrogs, for example, produce as many as 12,000 eggs each time they mate. That way, if a hunter eats some of the eggs, there are still likely to be some left.

This Cat-eyed Snake is dining on Red-eyed Tree Frog eggs. Tadpoles will soon develop inside any eggs the snake doesn't eat. When these baby frogs hatch, they'll drop into the stream below. Of course, there are hungry hunters in the water too. Fish, turtles, and water insects all eat baby frogs. So, once they hatch, baby frogs have to work at staying safe in order to grow up.

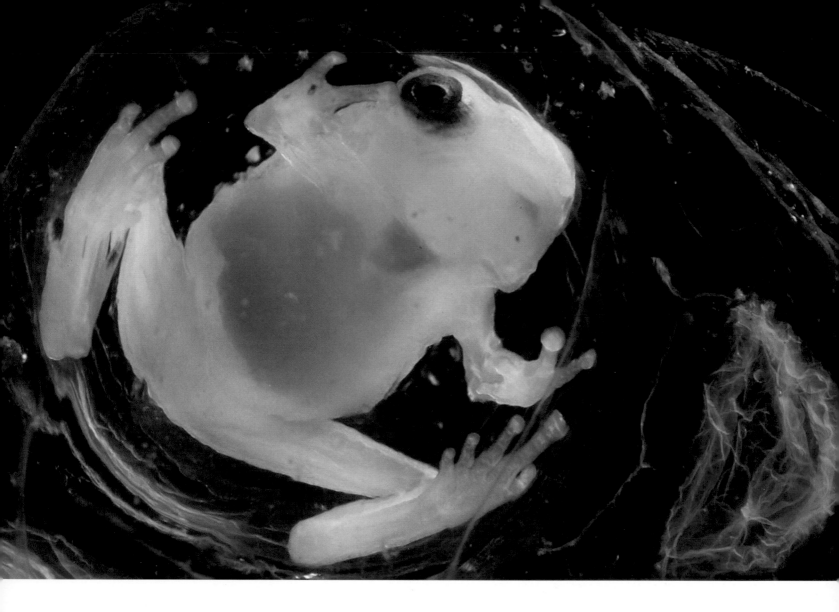

Two Ways to Grow Up

The bodies of all baby frogs change shape and function as they develop into adults. Some, like these Narrow-mouthed Frogs, change directly from a ball of cells into their adult form. Then the young adult frogs hatch.

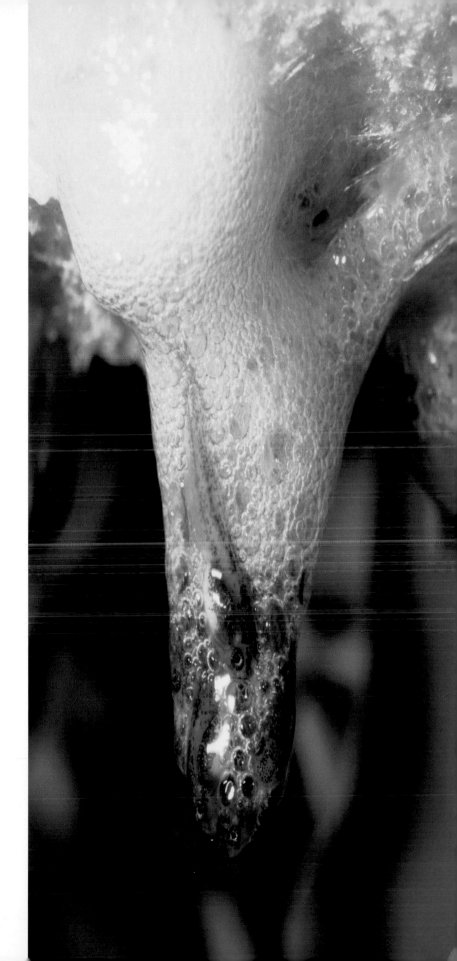

Most, though, go through a tad-pole stage. Take a close look at these Foam Nest Frog tadpoles. Each time a tadpole hatches, the liquid inside its egg spills into the foam nest. Because there are lots of eggs in a nest, hundreds of tadpoles hatch at the same time. So all the spilled liquid softens the dried foam. Drip! Drop! The softened bits of nest and the tadpoles start to drop out of the tree. That's why the frog parents stuck their nest to a branch just above the surface of a stream. The tadpoles land in the water. They'll finish growing up there.

ON THEIR OWN

Because most adult frogs leave their eggs once they are laid, most baby frogs grow up without parents. Some, like these Leaf Frog tadpoles, stay safe by remaining close to their brothers and sisters. Hunters are less likely to pick individuals out of a big group.

Some tadpoles have special features that help them stay safe. Torrent (TOR-ent) Frog tadpoles have really big lips. To stay alive, the tadpoles swim into the fastest-flowing part of the stream. Then they press their lips against rocks and use their mouths like suction cups to hold on. Carried along by the stream's rushing current, hungry fish zip past the tadpoles too fast to attack.

Baby Hourglass Tree Frogs appear to develop special body features only if they need them. So tadpoles living in ponds where there are few hungry hunters have skinny, see-through tails. But tadpoles living in ponds with lots of enemies look different. Those baby Hourglass Tree Frogs have thick, dark tails. Such a showy tail could distract an enemy. A baby frog could still grow up if all it lost were part of its tail. Losing its head would be another story.

Taking Care of Baby

Some baby frogs do get special care from their parents while they're growing up. This Strawberry Poison Dart Frog mother is giving her tadpole a ride to a special nursery—a pool of rainwater trapped in a plant's leaves. The mucus on her skin helps the baby frog hold on. Then she'll carry her other tadpoles, one at a time, to different nurseries. And her care doesn't end there. Every few days, the mother frog visits each of her tadpoles. While there, she produces a few eggs to deposit in the tadpole's pool. These eggs provide the baby frog with the food it needs to grow and change into an adult.

These young Darwin's Frogs have just hopped out of their father's mouth! During mating, the female lays about fifteen large eggs on top of damp leaves on the forest floor. The male stays close by, peeing on them to keep them wet until they hatch. Then he scoops the tadpoles into his mouth, where they slip into his *vocal sac,* the stretchy pouch covering his throat. For about two months, Dad gets on with his life, catching bugs to eat, while the tadpoles grow bigger. The baby frogs live on the food energy in the egg yolk they absorbed before they hatched. He can't make a sound with the tadpoles in his vocal sac, so having his brood become adults and hop out really gives him something to croak about!

These Hip Pocket Frog tadpoles are climbing up their father's legs. After the parents mate, the female deposits her eggs on leaf litter and leaves. Dad stands guard for about ten days, until the tadpoles hatch. Then he sits down in the middle of his brood so the tadpoles can wiggle into one of the pouches on his big hind legs. Although the female lays about twenty eggs, there is room only for about six tadpoles in each pouch. So only the strongest and fastest survive. Inside the pouches, the tadpoles grow and develop for about two months, living on the energy left from their egg yolks. When they change into young adults, they pop out of the pouches and hop away.

A baby frog that goes through a tadpole stage must change its shape to become an adult. It must also change the way its body works. While those changes don't happen all at once, most tadpoles become young adults in just a few months. Tadpoles in puddles that are drying up or those with a limited food supply change faster. The Strawberry Poison Dart Frog tadpole, growing up in its tiny rainwater pool, changes into an adult in just three weeks. On the other hand, a Bullfrog tadpole living in a big pond with plenty of food takes as long as fourteen months to become an adult. Even water temperature can affect how long it takes for tadpoles to develop— the colder the water, the longer it will take.

Fast or slow, the process of change is the same. Look closely at how this Wood Frog tadpole changes into an adult. One of the earliest changes is that bumps form and become hind legs.

Next, the tadpole grows front legs. Inside, its body is changing too. For one thing, the baby frog develops lungs. When the lungs take over the job of supplying oxygen, the young frog pokes its head out of the water and takes its first breath.

Soon the tadpole's fishlike body changes into its adult shape. Once eyelids develop, the youngster can blink. And the fishlike lips and mouth change into an adult frog's wide mouth and long tongue. Now the youngster is able to catch and digest insects.

Changing from a tadpole to a young adult frog takes lots of energy. Besides getting energy from the food it eats, the developing youngster uses up the food energy stored in its tail, making the tail shrink. Even before it's completely gone, though, the baby frog is ready for its life as an adult.

Where in the World Are These Frogs?

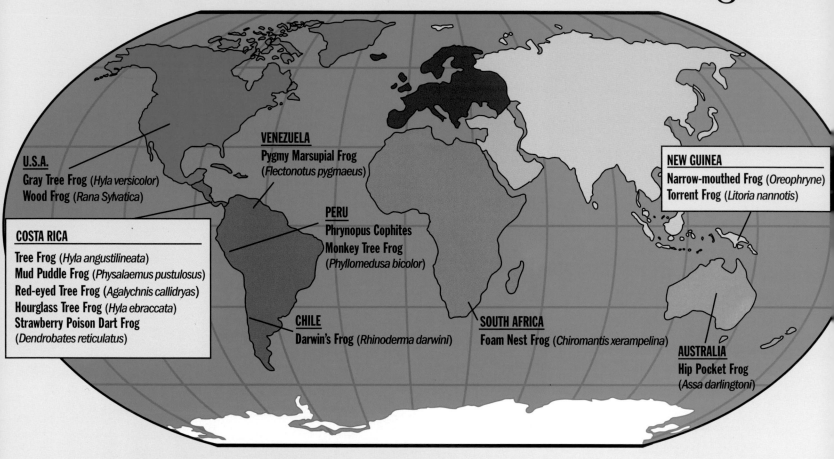

VENEZUELA
Pygmy Marsupial Frog
(*Flectonotus pygmaeus*)

NEW GUINEA
Narrow-mouthed Frog (*Oreophryne*)
Torrent Frog (*Litoria nannotis*)

U.S.A.
Gray Tree Frog (*Hyla versicolor*)
Wood Frog (*Rana Sylvatica*)

PERU
Phrynopus Cophites
Monkey Tree Frog
(*Phyllomedusa bicolor*)

COSTA RICA
Tree Frog (*Hyla angustilineata*)
Mud Puddle Frog (*Physalaemus pustulosus*)
Red-eyed Tree Frog (*Agalychnis callidryas*)
Hourglass Tree Frog (*Hyla ebraccata*)
Strawberry Poison Dart Frog
(*Dendrobates reticulatus*)

CHILE
Darwin's Frog (*Rhinoderma darwini*)

SOUTH AFRICA
Foam Nest Frog (*Chiromantis xerampelina*)

AUSTRALIA
Hip Pocket Frog
(*Assa darlingtoni*)

While the frogs you discovered in this book may also be found in other parts of the world, check the map to see where they were photographed.

In some parts of the world, frogs that were once common are now becoming rare. Researchers aren't sure why this is happening. Some suggest it's due to climate changes and diseases. Others think the cause is chemicals getting into the water, or wetlands being drained. More than likely, frog populations are being hurt by all of these things. Find out what kinds of frogs live in your area. Are any in trouble? If so, learn what is being done to protect them, and how your family can help. Then go to work to help save the frogs.

Raise Your Own Baby Frogs

Do frogs live in ponds or streams near you? If so, take some eggs home to watch them hatch and see the tadpoles change into frogs. Just follow these steps to care for the growing tadpoles. Then return the young frogs to the same place you collected the eggs. (Note: If frog populations in your area are shrinking, leave the eggs where you find them. Then visit every few days to look for tadpoles and see young adults emerge.)

1. Collect the eggs in a clean plastic container with a snap-on lid. Scoop up some water too so they don't dry out on the way home.

2. Put the eggs in a clean plastic or glass container with a wide opening. A fish bowl is perfect.

3. Fill the container with bottled water to be sure there are no chemicals, like chlorine and ammonia, which are bad for the baby frogs.

4. Add aquatic plants (available at stores that sell aquarium supplies). This will feed the tadpoles.

5. Lower the water level as soon as the tadpoles start to sprout legs. Also add rocks rinsed in bottled water so the young adults can climb. The frogs now need to breathe air.

6. Return the young frogs to their home as soon as their tails disappear.

GLOSSARY/INDEX

AMPHIBIAN [am-FIB-ee-an] A group of animals with gilled young that live in water and air-breathing adults that live at least part of the time on land. 4

EGG [eg] The name given to the female reproductive cell. It is also the name given to the fertilized egg that will produce a baby frog. 7, 8, 10, 11, 13, 15, 16, 21, 22, 24

GILL [gil] The body part in which oxygen is extracted from the water. 5

LUNG [lung] The body part in which oxygen is extracted from the air. 4, 28

MUCUS [MEW-kus] A thick, slippery fluid produced to moisten and protect the body part, such as the frog's skin, that produces it. 11, 21

OXYGEN [AHK-sih-jen] A gas in the air and water that passes into the tadpole's blood through the gills and into the adult's body through the lungs. The blood then carries it around the body, where it is combined with food to release energy. 4, 5, 7, 8, 28

SKIN [skin] The outer protective covering of a frog's body. 11

SPERM [spurm] The male reproductive cell. When the sperm joins with the female's egg, a baby frog develops. 7, 11

VOCAL SAC [VOH-kul sak] A pouchlike part in some kinds of male frogs. It swells up when the frog forces air from its lungs through it to produce sounds. 22

With love for Emily Sims McGrinder and her daughters: Kelly, Katie, Maura, Meghan, Molly, and Colleen

My favorite part of creating *Slippery, Slimy Baby Frogs* was finding the photos. Tracking down and contacting frog experts around the world was a detective job. I talked to one expert, through a satellite link, while he was deep in a Peruvian rain forest. After producing more than sixty photo-essays, I've made friends with many gifted wildlife photographers who spend their lives traveling to remote places and enduring difficult conditions to capture fantastic, once-in-a-lifetime shots. I'm delighted to share the images they work so hard to capture on film. Take another look at the photos in *Slippery, Slimy Baby Frogs* and you'll see a unique peek at young frogs taken by people who have made great efforts to study and photograph them.

Text copyright © 2006 by Sandra Markle

First published in the United States of America in 2006 by Walker Publishing Company, Inc.
Distributed to the trade by Holtzbrinck Publishers

For information about permission to reproduce selections from this book, write to Permissions, Walker & Company, 104 Fifth Avenue, New York, New York 10011

Library of Congress Cataloging-in-Publication Data

Markle, Sandra.
Slippery, slimy baby frogs / Sandra Markle.
  p. cm.
ISBN-10: 0-8027-8062-8 (hardcover)
ISBN-13: 978-0-8027-8062-1 (hardcover)
ISBN-10: 0-8027-8063-6 (reinforced)
ISBN-13: 978-0-8027-8063-8 (reinforced)
  1. Frogs—Infancy—Juvenile literature. I. Title.

QL668.E2M297 2006   597.8'9139—dc22
2005027542

Book design by Nicole Gastonguay

Visit Walker & Company's Web site at
www.walkeryoungreaders.com

Printed in China

10 9 8 7 6 5 4 3 2 1

Acknowledgment:
I would especially like to thank the following people for sharing their expertise and enthusiasm: Dr. Klaus Busse, Zoologisches Forschungsinstitut and Museum; Alexander Koenig, Bonn, Germany; Dr. Alessandro Catenazzi, Department of Biological Sciences, Florida International University; and Dr. Heike Proehl, Assistant Professor at the Institute of Zoology, Veterinary School of Hanover, Germany, specializing in the behavioral ecology of frogs. A special thank you to my husband, Skip Jeffery, for his help and support through the creative process.

Photo Credits:
Alessandro Catenazzi 10
Michael and Patricia Fogden cover, 6, 11, 12, 15, 16, 19, 20, 23
George Grall 1, 3, 5, 14, 17
Skip Jeffery 30
Dwight Kuhn 4, 26, 28, 29
Michael Mahony 25